SOLOMON'S WAY III

Copyright 2020 by Christopher J. Solomon
The book author retains sole copyright to
his contributions to this book.

Published 2020.
Printed in the United States of America.
All rights reserved.

No portion of this book may be reproduced, stored in a retrieval system, or transmitted in any form or by any means – electronic, mechanical, photocopy, recording, scanning, or other – except for brief quotations in critical reviews or articles, without the prior written permission of the author.

ISBN 978-1-950647-29-3

This book was published by BookCrafters,
Parker, Colorado.
www.bookcrafters.net

THE SECRETS OF SEDUCTIVE CONVERSATION

Christopher J. Solomon

DEDICATION

*To All Women
And the Men
Who Seduce Them*

ACKNOWLEDGEMENTS

I would like to acknowledge the Seducers of the past who have kept the game of Seduction alive and well all these years, and the Seducers of the present who shall keep the game of Seduction alive for the many years to come.

CONTENTS

Introduction..1
Chapter 1: Solomon's Rhetoric......................3
Chapter 2: First Words Spoken....................11
Chapter 3: Paving the Road to Bliss............23
Chapter 4: Igniting the Fire..........................45
Chapter 5: Melting the Sun..........................65
Chapter 6: Love Notes and Letters..............77
Chapter 7: Spell Casting..............................85
Chapter 8: Your Secret World......................97
Chapter 9: The Hypnotic Effect.................103
The Tenets of Solomon..............................111

INTRODUCTION

Women relish the entire courtship process, from first glance, to first touch, to first kiss, to first love-making session all the way to the first anniversary. But what gives all of these special moments that magical feeling, that deep and profound meaning, to women are the words spoken before and after these events.

The spoken word provides a pretext, a context, and a subtext to any otherwise uneventful event. And it is the spoken word that makes many a fair maiden swoon with delight into the arms of a skillful Seducer whose Silver Tongue knows no bounds.

Words help illuminate the darkest corners that actions alone only help to hide. Carefully constructed words work wonders to elevate reality above the mundane and into the world of fantasy and imagination. This is why women love words. Words are the fabric with which she weaves quilts, sheets, blankets, and comforters, all designed to make one feel safe, warm, and cared for. It is through her words bonds are created and fortified.

Words are also what frees her from herself, unleashes Her Inner Sex Goddess and allows her to indulge in the fantasy of her choosing (or your choosing). Therefore, it would be wise for a Master of Women to not only know how women are designed, but to also be adept at creating worlds she longs to hear about with your words.

In the pages that follow you will be guided through the secret world of Seductive Conversation, the elements that will allow you to soothe and caress women of your choosing with your words and more. You will move from knowing how to speak to knowing how to speak well in every encounter you have with women. You will be shown how to speak to parts of her that only the skillful know how to. Behold *Solomon's Way III: The Secrets of Seductive Conversation*.

Dr. Christopher J. Solomon
July 30, 2019

SOLOMON'S RHETORIC

"Of the many miles I have flown, none have been more fulfilling than the miles closest to your heart. What I imagined would be a journey of torture and torment from bad winds and rain was instead a journey paved with pleasure from sunny days. It is a must that my lips kiss your petals and my tongue taste your nectar."
— Seducer Bee, to his Sweet Flower

Many men have found themselves surprisingly victorious in the game of Seduction by spouting words they never knew they had or speaking thoughts they never thought they could, while others have failed simply because they knew not the words to say when the time was appropriate. Although everyone has their ideas about what's correct in every situation, perhaps clarification is in order at least within the realm of Seduction.

In the realm of Seduction, great care must be taken so one does not become the object of one's own Seduction. This could easily come about when one is at a loss for words and naturally brings the topic of conversation to oneself. Nothing could be worse in the realm of Seduction, yet this is what is suggested by so-called-masters to those who feel a lull in the conversation or nervousness. This is the death of the Seductive Aura.

What should be applied and understood by any man who wishes to seduce women is that it is his duty as well as his right to lay siege to the woman, or women, he deems worthy of his companionship. Sure, nerves may seem to get the best of you at times, but this extra energy should be used to energize your pursuits, not sway you away from them. Therefore, once it is understood that speaking about yourself is a recipe for disaster, and sometimes nerves may distract you, you still have the right to go for what you desire. And to help you hone your silver tongue, I shall now introduce you to a tried and true Seductive Device we shall call Solomon's Rhetoric.

Solomon's Rhetoric is the magic formula that bridges the gap between linguistics, psychology, and pleasure within the human brain. Traditional Rhetoric is the art of "effectively using language in speech or writing, or the use of exaggerated language, bombast." Solomon's Rhetoric is more of the same except its use is to induce a Seductive State in the opposite sex. What sets this language apart from any other language construct is that words which define specifics are used less, and general terms are used more, hence engaging the imagination. Also, sentence length is longer and contains more syllables. Sentence structure is based on the correct number of syllables which tap into the frequency within the brain responsible for pleasure and happiness. The words become notes which are carefully composed to create symphonies. For example, a statement such as, "I like your earrings," given the rhetorical treatment becomes, "I admire your embellishments."

The elements contained within Solomon's Rhetoric are Alliteration, Imagery, Metaphors, Prepositions, Modals, The Subjunctive Mood, Sentence Length, and the General feel of the Victorian Era with a sense of Timelessness.

Alliteration is the repetition of a sound at the beginning of words. First and foremost, saying something unintentionally unexpected would definitely define your dream's desire and would be a sentence full of alliteration. This formation naturally delights the ears and so any message is happily accepted even if the message is non-sensical as above.

Imagery is what takes the mind away from the normal mundane aspects of human situations and elevates them to a place where anything is possible. The greatest faculty within our brain is the imagination. Although in real life we rarely have the time to explore our imagination, the brain is naturally inclined to accept any image imbued or anything that would induce imagery and spark the imagination. "To stare at the red rose's raindrop..."

Metaphors enhance the meaning of simple subjects therefore bringing about properties not readily apparent in the subject itself. This is usually done with the help of imagery whose aspect relates to the simple subject. A woman walking to your dwelling in the rain could say, "I walked in the rain to get here." Or she could say, "I have swum an ocean for you and would do so much more, but what the waters have taken from me I trust that you will restore."

Prepositions help introduce a thought by giving your

words a sense of substance. Prepositions of location work well in breathing life into topics. These include but are not limited to the following: off, on, in, to, beneath, near, below, besides, under, over, and across. For example, "Beneath the starlight is where you must've been born." Or "Of all the places your light could shine, it had to shine into my dark and decrepit soul."

Modals help take your words out of the world of fact and into the world of hypotheticals by suggesting conditions like need, ability, probability, obligation, likelihood and permission. Modal words are: could, can, may, might, should, shall, would, must, ought to and used to. Although not a modal, the word "if" is used to enter the world of possibility also. Modals are suggestive and connotative and used in connotative and in combinations to convey such things as contingencies, possibilities, needs, requirements and abilities.

The Subjunctive mood is the "expression" of wishes, contingencies, conjectures, desires, recommendations, requirements, uncertainties, or anything else contrary to fact. In this respect, its uses resemble that of a modal verb, and modals are often used in Subjunctive constructions: "If only I could become whole again," or "I wish your light weren't so blinding." The spoken word in the Subjunctive Mood is rarely used nowadays.

Sentence length is one of the defining features of Solomon's Rhetoric. Simply put, there are no short sentences, at least none shorter than eight syllables. The reason behind this madness is women take in more from your speech than just the content. They glean the meaning of what you're saying not only from the words you speak, but also from how you are speaking them. The longer you can enrapture her with your spiel, the longer time she has to fantasize about you and what you can do to her. Women long to be dominated by words so bind her the way she wants to be bound.

To give the general feel of the Victorian Era and a sense of timelessness, a certain mindset is in order. The Victorian Era was the time in Europe when men wore suits, vests, hats, with canes and pocket watches, and women wore corsets, long flowing dresses, arm-length gloves, fans and umbrellas. Although one not need to dress like this, one does need to understand that the subtext during this time was carnal bliss, where the man played the gentleman and the women responded in kind by fanning themselves or otherwise playing coy until it was time to tear each other's clothes off and rip into each other's flesh like wild beasts. It was a game, it was theater at its best, and it was the time humanity remembers as the best for courtship and romance. It was the secret world men and women enjoyed the most. The beautiful fair maiden in public was the super-sex goddess behind closed doors. No time or place was off limits. Desire was the goal.

This should be the quality that distinguishes you from the rest. No task shall be so important as that of pleasuring your woman. She shall know that when you are around her, she could be pleasured at anytime, anywhere. Being guided by your desire for her immediately makes you timeless and romantic to the females of our species.

Be not deluded into thinking that speaking with literary flair is not needed or is too soft to be effective. Women love any effort put forth in the realm of romance. Also, another thing to keep in mind is that men and women speak different languages, even though both may use the same words.

A man's primary purpose in speaking is to impart some sort of information while a woman's primary purpose for speaking is to share or bond. Therefore, the male cannot use the same words he uses with his male friends on a woman. The effect will not be the same. A woman can speak to a man with her language, but again the effect will not be the same. If she expects him to have the same responses as her friends, she will be disappointed.

The mid-line for communicating differently to the female of our species is Solomon's Rhetoric and that of the like. It is a man's duty to display his feathers in much the same way a peacock displays its feathers. Although physical displays have their place, much more can be gained through verbal displays.

It must also be understood that one not need speak entirely in Solomon's Rhetoric at every turn. Not at all. A few choice sentences at the service of excellence
is all that is needed.

The chapters that follow will detail the complete construction and dissection of the Seductive conversation.

USE YOUR WORDS EFFECTIVELY

FIRST WORDS SPOKEN

"𝔗omes speak not of how fortunate 𝔍 have been to have caught your gaze from across the garden."
Drakkulus to Prudence
in *Prudence*, a romance novel.

Many men often believe that the embers of desire begin with the first words spoken. This is sometime true, but more often than not, the sparks begin long before words exit your mouth. This is the way things have been for our species long before the invention of language and the spoken word. This is not to say the spoken word doesn't play a part nowadays. It most certainly does. Just know that from a biological standpoint nature instilled within us mechanisms to receive desire.

All has been detailed in the first volume of the series *Solomon's Way: The Ancient Secrets and Methods of a Seducer*, but in case this volume was passed over in favor for the current one, then an explanation is in order.

CHRISTOPHER J. SOLOMON

The signal that males send to females of the human species in order to let them know that they are interested in them is known as the Copulatory Gaze. The Copulatory Gaze is the oldest mating signal in existence and is foolproof. Simply put, if the woman of your desires sends the correct signal back within 3 seconds, you are to approach her as you have been given the green light. This green light is as old as time itself and pretty much invites whatever production you can produce for her. But of course, one must respect social decorum and proceed as a gentleman with a short leash on his desire.

Once you are given the green light and you approach, the first words spoken should be to greet her and introduce yourself. Not much thought should be given to this as "Hello, my name is" should suffice. She should in turn give you her name in kind. In centuries past, it was proper for a woman to raise her hand to the gentleman to whom she was being introduced. Some women do this instinctively, some do not. Regardless, the point is not to shake it like some sort of buffoon but to take it within your hand and lightly kiss the back of it. If she does show an effort to raise her hand, this is what you shall do while looking into her eyes. Say the words "It is a pleasure to meet you." If no effort is given, then take her hand yourself and proceed as above.

This is how a Seducer greets a fair maiden, especially one he wishes to subdue. Her instincts will tell her that you are charming enough to notice her as a woman, but it is after this point many men falter. The correct structure to follow for the Seducer is: Method, introduction and intention. We have taken care of the first two steps. It is the intention men either get wrong or don't care to signal.

SOLOMON'S WAY III

    This throws things into an awful state of confusion because a woman expects to be wooed especially by any suitor within her immediate vicinity. To have carried forth with the first two parts of the equation, but not the last, is the reason many women complain to their girlfriends about men not catching their signals. Again, women don't want to have to spell it out for you. You should be enraptured with the female of our species enough to do your "homework." But of course, many are either too busy for "homework" or are not cognizant that "homework" exists.

    But fear not, the work has been done for you and here it is: She wants you to announce your intentions early on so that she knows how to regard you. This is easily done after you have told her it was a pleasure meeting her by saying something simple such as, "You look like someone I would like to get to know better. I would like to call you tonight." Or "You look absolutely intoxicating. I wouldn't be able to sleep tonight if I couldn't call you." These are words she longs to hear, so say them.

    A woman wants to know you find her not only beautiful, but also ravishing enough for you to put yourself on the front line in the race for her desire. This flatters the females of our species. It is the reason they doll themselves up with the clothes, the hair, the make-up, the perfume, the lipstick, etc. She would hate to see that all of her effort to attract a mate was pointless in the long run, but would be absolutely charmed to know that her hard work paid off.

    She doesn't know what you want with her until you tell her. She doesn't want to have to guess at it. Men often think that it is the woman who puts the man in the friend zone. This is not true. It is the man who puts himself in the friend zone by not announcing his intention. If she does not know that you have anything to offer in regard to her pleasure and happiness, how will she ever know how to assist you in winning her over? It is the man's duty to provide the foundation on which her pleasure is built; the foundation on which anything is possible.

Many men think that they are coming in under the radar by posing as a friend first. They also think that from this standpoint as a friend they will somehow bridge the gap from friend to lover in one fell swoop. Women aren't that naive to not know what you are up to. They may just like you enough to make you feel you're pulling a fast one on her.

While achievement has been had with this method, it is lowly and definitely not the way of the Seducer. The Seducer has no qualms or hang-ups about his desire for women. And believe it or not, women also don't have any qualms or hang-ups about his desire for women. Women actually love that a man can become so engorged with desire for them that he puts nothing else above his desire for them.

Be not fooled by outside influences into thinking that announcing your desire for women is wrong in any way. This is how you came about. Of course, women also respect social decorum and their reputations, but that is about it. Speak to her the way she wants you to, and you shall inherit riches you never thought you would.

Digressions aside, the last part of the equation is to announce your intention. Paying her a compliment always plays well as she will know that you noticed her. Women love to be noticed. It is encoded in their DNA to stand out somehow so that the opposite sex will notice.

SOLOMON'S WAY III

Once you have employed the method, introduced yourself, and announced your intention, you could end the interaction because you have her number, or because one or both of you have pressing engagements, or you could stay and extend the interaction by having a conversation. This is also where many men falter as they know not what to say. First and foremost, it should be understood that nothing is so important that it must be spoken a certain way, correctly, with perfection. The interaction isn't so great that your next spoken words must be completely important. It is just conversation. The fact that you have been given. the green light and have done what was necessary to put yourself on the frontline is enough and far ahead of everyone else in the race for her desire. All that is needed now is for you to relax and to get her relaxed. The way you do this is by staying focused on her.

When you bring the spotlight on her, she gets to put on a production for you in order to reward your efforts in announcing your intention. Ask her questions about herself that begin with what, why, where, who, when, and how. Follow up what she says by paraphrasing. Adding utterances such as uh-huh, huh, and mmm shows that you're listening and allows her to continue speaking. When there is a break in the conversation, stare into her eyes silently. Then, pay her a compliment such as, "When you smile, the light turns your eyes into shimmering diamonds." After enough of these or even just one, you can and should go in for a kiss. It must be understood that you do not ask questions with the humanless intent of an interviewer or reporter.

The main thing you should do is listen. Actually, listen to what she is saying. Uncover parts of her from the words she uses, words she doesn't use, intentions behind her words. Flesh out her character, who she is, who she wants to become. Find out what makes her tick, what makes her unique. The point of your conversation is to not only find out about her, but to make her feel understood and validated.

Once you make her feel validated and understood, by reflecting back to her who she is, what she desires, and her view of things, you will see an unmistakable glow come over her., This is Her Inner Sex Goddess being awakened. It is during this time her pupils will dilate and her breathing will become heavy. At this point you could and should definitely go in for the kiss.

Some men forgo the method all together and go straight for speaking first. This is okay and at a certain rate has its success, but the trouble with this approach is men often don't know what to say or they end up saying something stupid. All they know is something must be said at any and all costs. This is great as instinct has done its job. But we cannot rely on instinct alone. We must also rely on intelligence to structure our instinct in a way to ensure success.

So, if one wishes to subdue a beautiful woman, but the method cannot be employed, there is still a way to succeed, although the words you use must contain more substance as you have not been given. the green light. So, this becomes the goal: The green light.

There are no such things as pick-up lines in the realm of Seduction. Pick-up lines weren't meant to be taken seriously or actually meant to be used to seduce women. They are meant to be humorous comments with the male/female interplay as their topic. Do not try to succeed using pick-up lines. Your tragedy will be horrible.

SOLOMON'S WAY III

The correct way to initiate conversation without any pretext beforehand is to make a comment, compliment, an observation, or to ask a question. The perfect way for a Seducer would be to give a compliment, then to ask a question. Of course, any of the above could work alone or in unison with each other. For example, an observation then a question, then a compliment. One of the best is to ask a woman for her opinion on something. This bodes well when it comes to validation.

A woman's opinion or point of view is never held in the same esteem as a man's opinion. So, when she hears that you want her opinion on something, she feels heard, valued, and validated.

The topic or topics you chose to converse about should revolve eventually around her. Sometimes it may be necessary to speak about other topics such as observations, headlines, or current events so as not to seem too intrusive. Asking opinions about these things allows you to probe further into who she is. Once the conversation has gone back and forth between you two at least three times, then it will be proper to introduce yourself and greet her as you would under normal circumstance. This immediately shows your intention and doesn't have her wondering how to regard you.

The fact that she was willing to extend the conversation shows that she is at least somewhat interested in what you have to say. This does not mean that she has an interest in you in any sense. This must be understood, because many men are disappointed when they misinterpret this slight conversation as sexual interest. She could just be friendly, bored or whatever. How she reacts to your introduction will tell you if you have been given the green light.

If after you kissed the back of her hand, and she asked you about your girlfriend or/and your wife, then she is interested. If she asked you personal questions that you wouldn't generally ask a stranger, then she is interested. You have been given the green light. She will also let you know if she is spoken for either by casually mentioning her husband or boyfriend or just by telling you immediately that she is taken.

If you are not given the green light it would be a waste of your time to persist, especially when you could be spending your time on a woman more receptive to your charms. It may seem like a challenge to persist, to see if you could overcome her resistance, but more often than not, you will just come off as creepy, pushy, and needy.

If she gives you the green light yet mentions a boyfriend or husband, and gives you the attention as if she's single, you should persist until she resists as you just may succeed. Sometimes they really don't have boyfriends or husbands. They say that to seem like a forbidden fruit. And sometimes they do have boyfriends and husbands, but if they don't seem to care, why should you?

Contact should be made as quickly as possible so as not to make a big deal out of it later on. It takes the awkwardness out of touching each other later.

The point in this phase is not only to make contact with her, but to also show her that you can hold your own in conversation. Communicating with women puts them at ease with you and allows them to feel safe and secure in your presence.

You do not want to steal the spotlight from her. It is her show. She may ask about you. You should keep your answers short and turn the attention back to her.

SOLOMON'S WAY III

When you listen, be sure to give her your undivided attention. This means making eye contact, looking at her lips and back to her eyes. This is called adoring her. Women love to look good and thus, love to be looked at. Remember: cool, calm and collected.

You should allow aspects of your personality to show through, but of course, great caution must be taken in revealing your sense of humor in great amounts too soon in your Seduction. The point is to have your woman see you as the strong romantic type, not the class clown or dancing monkey. It is quite fine to make her laugh, but not cool her down. You are trying to warm her up. Being the entertainment will quickly douse any flame that you worked so hard to get started. And once the fire is out, that is when you have effectively put yourself in the friend zone.

The correct way to display personality and sense of humor is to tease her, touch her, make her laugh, but never let her forget that your intention is to make her yours. She will honor your efforts and tender herself as the reward.

WISDOM IS WHAT YOU KNOW

PAVING THE ROAD TO BLISS

A charming devil can only be a charming devil if he can produce the charm. Otherwise he is just a devil. Every Seducer must have something to talk about. This does not mean that he talks non-stop at every instance. Not at all. Nothing can ruin a Seduction more than a man who thinks it is necessary to fill every silence with words of his own. And being a chatter box is anything but attractive to women who want you to possess them. What this means is that you shall not speak of anything at length that is not conducive to the Seduction, but you must possess and always have at your disposal a treasure box of subjects that you know and know well.

These subjects include but are not limited to the following: <u>Stories, jokes, tricks, wisdom, proverbs, knowledge of historical events, psychology, divination, and skill sets</u>. Out of these nine subjects a Seducer must know a minimum of three from each category. In each and every Seduction, a minimum of four of the nine subjects should be covered in order to hold and maintain a spell-binding conversation. This strategy ensures that you will never be at a loss for words. Also, what this does is allows the Seducer to create his own ways in which to enchant and show your fair lady that you are a knowledgeable and competent suitor worthy of her charms. After you have been successful in many Seductions, you can and should build yourself a repertoire of what works best for you.

While only three from each group is all that is required, a true Master Seducer has more than ten of each category at his disposal. This is what a Seducer sharpens and enhances in his time alone when there are no women present to test his might. What good is a beautiful sword if it does not cut? Practice is a must.

Before we journey into examples of the subjects above, it must be understood that your purpose is to show your lady a good time while in your presence. If she does not enjoy herself, she will not want to carry on a conversation with you nor have another with you in the future. You are to display charm and wit while at the same time never losing focus on your intention or your goal.

Although any of the subjects mentioned could be used alone with success, it is good to show that you are versatile and know many things that could delight her. Also, it is paramount that you are able to carry forward with your campaign if and when your subjects do not take hold as they should. Remain calm. Make light of it by adding humor or simply move on to another subject. The point is to engage her, not for you to be the primary focus of your Seduction. You

SOLOMON'S WAY III

should create a world where it is only you two and no one else and nothing else matters.

While bringing forth these subjects be sure to bring the spotlight back to her: Ask her questions, what she thinks about so and so and so forth and so on. Women thrive on interaction so give her something to thrive on.

STORIES

Your stories could be about you, someone you know or just something you heard or read. The best stories for women are those that involve a female character and some emotion. Women automatically identify with the female of any story so she can feel what she feels. This is often the reason women love romantic comedies and dramas and why they are able to cry over a character in a movie or book. The best kind of stories a Seducer can tell are either cute based, love based, or lust based. You do not want to bother with gross or asinine stories. She is judging you, and if you tell disgusting stories that's how she will view you. By that same token if you tell cute, lovely, or lusty stories, this is how she will view you.

When it comes to cute based stories, the best ones should come from your childhood.

It could be about how your dog ran away and you cried for a week, and after posting signs everywhere, you went to the pound and there he was. Or how in the 5th grade you had a crush on a girl so you decided to write her a poem inspired by a Dr. Seuss book, or how you didn't have a girlfriend until the 10th grade. What matters more in this field is sharing yourself with her, but be sure to touch and go. Bring up your stories in order to ask about her, to find out if she's ever experienced anything like that. You are bonding.

When it comes to love based, you could speak of yourself or someone else. Just be sure to emphasize the components of love in the story. What he or she did for love, how they showed love, what they sacrificed for love, what the result of their love was, etc. Then, ask her what she thinks. A woman will tell you all that you need to know in matters regarding the heart. All you have to do is listen.

When it comes to lusty stories, the point is not to gross her out, freak her out, or make her feel uncomfortable. The point is to open up her mind to what she likes and to make sure she likes them with you. You must tread carefully with lusty stories as there is a very fine line between being Seductive and attractive and being plain creepy. You should always gauge how she is reacting to your words. If she doesn't seem to grow defensive, or doesn't change the subject, pursue. You can begin by telling her a story you heard of a woman who was 23, but never experienced an orgasm. If she comments on it but doesn't shut you down, you can go to describe her features, where she lived, and a man she met at the coffee shop. One day she invited him over to her house for some coffee and his hand brushed her knee under the table. It sent electricity through her body. And when he left, she took a shower and using the shower head she experienced her first orgasm. This story can go any way you want it to. It doesn't matter so long as her imagination is being engaged. If you see her becoming more relaxed, and her breathing becomes heavy and deep, you can be sure your words have done their job in arousing her. You don't want to use a story from your life in these stories as again, she'll judge you and more than likely see you as slimy and creepy. You also do not want to be seen as trying too hard to be attractive. Although she may feel that you are successful with many women does not mean she wants to hear the details of your affairs.

When you tell stories, make sure to make them engaging and to ask your lady how or if they apply to her. This will make you a Master story teller.

JOKES

Jokes take on a different structure in the realm of Seduction. Normally, anything that could get a laugh is a joke and is worthy for any audience. This is not so in Seduction. In Seduction, your jokes should be funny and flirty. Crass or disgusting jokes ruin a Seductive atmosphere. Unless she offers a joke of her own that breaks the line of what is deemed appropriate, keep your jokes within the realm of safety by making them funny and flirty.

It should be understood that what a man considers funny is not the same thing a woman generally considers funny. You can find many jokes out there that would appeal to women like the following: Two old men are sitting on a park bench. One says, "I love my wife. She always cooks for me after we make love. What about you?" The other guy says, "Yeah, I know what you mean. She cooked me meatloaf, twice." You should not rely too much on jokes as you do not want to come off as a clown or comedian. It is good to be able to crack jokes here and there, but you are not doing a stand-up comedy. There are many categories men enter unknowingly that puts them in the friend zone, and being a comedian is one of them. Tread lightly when it comes to jokes.

TRICKS

Nothing has a more spellbinding effect beyond words than Magic tricks. To fool an on-looker into thinking you possess some sort of communion with a force greater than mankind, has been a great source of gratification for many magicians and a great source of reverence for on-lookers. The allure of the occult and the Dark Arts has always attracted those who are for and against them. The world would be bland without a little mystery, so it would be worth your time and effort to learn at least three good magic tricks. Also, you can use the tricks below handcrafted for our purposes.

The first trick is called "Pick a Number." All you need to perform this trick is a writing instrument and paper to write. Tell your woman to pick a number between one and 500, but not to tell you what it is. Give her a few seconds to do so.

Then ask her if she's got it. When she says "Yes," look her deep in the eyes then underneath the cover of your hand, write the following on the paper: You're intoxicating, I just needed to see you smile when you read this. Then fold it up and ask her what number she chose. When she tells you, slide the paper to her in all seriousness as if you got it right. When she reads it, smiles and looks at you, you've done your job.

This next trick is called, "Now you see it, not you don't." This one requires a little preparation, a little practice, and a little acting. You will need two identical

SOLOMON'S WAY III

small square sheets of paper, no larger than two inches square. On one of these squares write "Magic may have blinded me, but it is your beauty that gives me sight." Then crumple this sheet into a small paper ball and place it within your left jacket pocket or back left pants pocket. When you are ready to perform, take out the blank sheet of paper and a pen.

Tell your lady that you want to show her something. Pretend to write something on the face of the paper out of the view of your woman. You can do this in front of her, but be sure your other hand covers what you are supposedly writing. When you are done writing, crumple the paper into a small paper ball as the one before. Take the paper ball into your right fingertips where your woman can see it. Get right next to her where her right shoulder is close enough to touch your left shoulder. Tell her, "I can make this disappear by touching it to my left palm three times. Watch."

Open your left hand and start by touching the paper ball to your left palm. Then, raise it to your right ear and back down to your left palm and say "One." Be sure to keep your eyes locked on your left palm even when you move your right hand. Lift the paper ball back to your right ear and back down to your left palm saying "Two." Lift the paper ball back to your right ear, except on the way to your ear, open your fingers so the ball is released behind the both of you. Be sure no one is there to get hit or tell on you. Also, make this movement as subtle as possible because it is the whole trick. And be sure not to look at your woman to see if she caught it. If you keep your eyes on your left palm, she will too. When you bring your right hand back down to your left palm, quickly close your left hand and say "Three."

Then look at your left fist as if it has the paper ball there. Then, make magical gesture with your right hand open over your left, the slowly open your left hand to show that the ball has vanished.

This of course will make her smile, and she'll make guesses as to what you've done with it. If you have tossed it far enough there will be no trace of it anywhere. Then she's convinced that it is gone, turn to your left and point to your right ear and say, "It's behind my ear." As soon as you turn to point and speak, as subtle as possible reach into your jacket or pants pocket to retrieve the ball of paper you wrote on earlier. Hold it in your fingers lightly, but to where she can't see it.

Then say, "It's actually behind your ear." Then reach behind her right ear, grazing her ever so slightly with your left hand holding the hidden ball and produce the paper ball for her to see. Once she sees it, give it to her and say, "Here. Open it." Let her read it. End of trick. From here you could go in for the kiss as your reward or just because she's beautiful. Or you could continue to charm her.

The trick above is real magic or advanced sleight-of-hand, but with practice you will get it.

The last trick that can be used to charm and delight is a variation of the first, except this one is different. You don't need a piece of paper or pen. Simply say

"You know, I have been known to be a little psychic. Watch." And with your most serious facial expression close your eyes, touch your temple and say, "Think of a number between one and..." pause for dramatic effect then say "Three."

If she has a good head on her shoulders, then she should laugh at your ridiculousness, but if she doesn't, because she doesn't realize the simplicity of your verbal trick, then give her the answer "Two" and pretend you knew it all along. If she truly was fooled, then you are wasting too much effort to Seduce her.

Again, you should not rely on tricks in order to Seduce. This should only be a weapon in your arsenal. You want to present things as a whole, not just a part as you could easily become a dancing monkey which is what you do not want.

WISDOM

Women are inherently attracted to knowledge, and if a man happens to come her way who possesses some kind of knowledge, then she will more than likely be attracted to him. The reasoning behind this madness is biological.

A woman expects a man to lead. She expects to be able to trust in him with her life, her kids, her everything. The only way she can do this is by seeing the confidence within his soul. This confidence comes from his possession of knowledge that is tried and true, thereby becoming wisdom. A man who possesses wisdom is far ahead of everyone else in the race for her heart, as he knows the effect of what he knows.

There are many ways one can project wisdom. You can simply state it depending on the circumstances as in, "You should eat something before you drink. That way you will have more tolerance because the alcohol will not be the only thing in your bloodstream." Or you could simply state something you recently heard, read, or learned. "If you want to get your money's worth on a drink, order your beverage without ice. When they bring you your drink, politely ask for a cup of ice or get your own ice. Ice can take up to half of the volume of the cup so you end up paying more for less." Your wisdom doesn't necessarily have to be geared to these topics. The point is to be able to offer some sort of insight that wasn't present without your assistance or offering.

PROVERBS

Offering proverbs to frame a situation, or just as a topic of conversation, is another way you can prove your worth by offering wisdom. The difference between just offering wisdom and proverbs is with wisdom you're not quoting anyone or yourself. You're just offering some knowledge. With proverbs, you are directly quoting someone who said something that either applies to the situation or holds a bunch of conversational value. You don't necessarily have to offer up someone else's quote, you can offer up your own quotes. Just know that you should say your own quotes as if someone else said them, and only reveal you are the creator after you are asked. The reason is you don't want to seem like you're stealing someone else's material, nor do you want to seem needy for approval or recognition. This can easily happen if you follow or lead with, "Here's a proverb I created" or "I created that." Just say "A wise man once said..." and be done with it. See where the conversation leads. Here are some of my favorite proverbs: "A wise man once said something wise. Something about lemons and lemonade. I hope that helps," "Sometimes hardships are necessary in order to make you stronger than you were before," and "The right eye cannot always see what the left eye can perceive." I created those, really.

SOLOMON'S WAY III

KNOWLEDGE OF HISTORICAL EVENTS

Being a well-rounded individual or a skillful Seducer means having an arsenal that contains many weapons. One of these weapons, in conjunction with the others, that will show you to have an interesting and timeless quality is a working knowledge of historical events. The things you speak about are what affects you and moves you emotionally the most. You can easily define someone's character based on what topics they choose to talk about. Also, much wisdom is gained by listening to how someone speaks about the topics they choose. So choose your topics wisely. If you speak about war, the holocaust, slavery and complain about how terrible these things were, you will come across as anything but a Seducer. Sure, these things may inspire you to great diatribes worthy of a TV special, but they will not inspire the woman you are speaking with to want to continue a conversation with you.

Arguing with the fairer sex definitely has its place, and it's fun when the topics are light and the sparks ignited can lead to a nice romantic fire. But it is terrible, to say the least, when the topics bring on personal attacks and cause pain, anger, and emotions that lead to resentment whose sparks ignite wildfires.

You do not want to push your woman away, nor do you want her to secretly resent you or hate you. You want to make her feel that she *can* talk to you about anything; that if a topic is brought up, you won't be judgmental and critical; that you know how to navigate your way through topics you've never encountered before.

You can show her all of this by bringing up an event

from history, usually ten years or better, and give insights from three perspectives: those who were for such actions, those who were against such actions, and your perspective on the actions or events that took place. For instance, the Trojan War. Some would say the Trojan War was brought about because of Helen of Troy as she did run away with Paris. But later, the skillful Rhetorician Gorgias displayed what could be brought up in her defense if one actually tried to clear her. This could go on in any direction you like. Or you could mention Marquis De Sade wrote all of his novels from a prison cell and where we get the term Sadist. Or how Casanova seduced even nuns during his reign as a Seducer. Just remember it is not only the topic you bring up, but also how you choose to speak about them that matters. If you wish to change your perspective on how you view things, change the words you use to describe them.

PSYCHOLOGY

In this field, you must not only be able to speak about human psychology, you must also be a master of human psychology. You would do yourself a great injustice by doing work someone else has already done for you. We as a human species have been around for quite some time, and along the way, man noticed certain patterns that could be condensed into general principles. This is what psychology does. It breaks down human thoughts, actions, and behaviors so you can not only understand the people around you better but can also understand yourself better.

Trying to convince or persuade anyone of anything

SOLOMON'S WAY III

seems like it should be as simple as stating facts and using logic. Only in a perfect world would this approach work. But we do not live in a perfect world, nor do we operate off logic the way we should. Therefore, there are many other things you need to be aware of that can make your job easier.

For instance:

- If you want someone to be receptive to your ideas, it is better to speak to them while the two of you are moving. Physiology can play a big part in letting an idea in or keeping an idea out.
- Everyone hates to stand in line for something so if you offer an idea, make sure it is short, quick, and to the point. The longer the steps, the more complex, the longer the line you have just created in the listener's mind.
- If you want someone to tell you what they really think about something, don't just ask them what they think. Ask them how they would do it or improve it.
- People naturally want to tell the truth. It is how the human species is designed. People have to work and train to tell a lie as good as the truth. You can gauge someone's baseline behavior by asking them something that requires the truth. Then, watch how calm or relaxed they are. How they respond behavior-wise is their baseline behavior. Then, ask them to tell you three things. Two of these things must be true and one must be a lie. Tell them they can do it in any order they like and you're going to try to spot the lie. If you see their eyes shift, they start to twitch, prolong eye contact, move their limbs

and/or tense up, this is all due to stress within the gross vehicle which means a lie has been told.
- You can get anyone to be forthcoming with information by assuming that you already know the answer and revealing it to• them, regardless if it is true or not. Humans have an inherent need to tell the truth, to be correct, and to correct those who are wrong. So, by giving false information, the person you are talking to will feel the need to correct you by giving you the correct information if they have it.
- Women wear eye make-up and lipstick to make their eyes and lips stand out to the opposite sex. They do this on purpose so compliment them.

These psychological tidbits can be discussed with whomever you wish or deem worthy of such knowledge, but you should also try to enhance your psychological knowledge by reading and studying the world of psychology. There are many avenues and fields that span several volumes. The tidbits I mention here are barely sprinkles of water from the great ocean that makes up psychology.

DIVINATION

This area falls into the realm of the Dark Arts and runs well with tricks and psychology. Divination is being able to give some sort of display of communion with a Supernatural entity, or your being a possessor of Supernatural ability who can detail someone's past or future. This takes

SOLOMON'S WAY III

the form of Mediums, who communicate with "Dead People," Psychics, Palm Readers, etc. The key is based in psychology which states that everyone's favorite subject is themselves. Therefore, you should speak about the person, and you should speak well about them.

People, regardless if you know they are good or bad, will always resonate with good traits and overlook or ignore the bad traits. Also, as stated above, people will tend to correct you if you are wrong, and once they give you some truth about their lives or who they are, all you have to do is state it later on in your own words. The point is to come across as mystical. Women may not say it outwardly, but they love the Darkside and anything that is mystical has endless Seductive appeal. You can state your claims as entertainment, or you could just include it with your persona. A Seducer who can speak to a woman's soul is one who will have many successes under his belt.

For example, you can tell your woman this, "I can tell by the way you're holding your glass in front of you that you've been let down by men in the past..." and let her fill in the blanks. You also want to tell her, "You are very smart when it comes to revealing yourself to others." This is an old weapon of many Seducers of the past.

The "Mad Monk" Rasputin was a consummate seducer who used Divination and Spiritual trappings to entice and seduce his women. He told his women things about themselves no one else knew, and he showed the world things they never thought were possible. This realm should be handled with care as there are still very many people out there who take this subject, and the things in it, very seriously and believe in them without a doubt. Be sure if you use Divination in your repertoire that you are ready to have a following as a result.

Skillset

Lastly, we come to the final weapon in the Seducer's bag of tricks. A Skillset is something you can do well enough to call a skill. You can know the value of your skill based on whether or not anyone is willing to pay you for it. If so, however miniscule, then it is a skill. The amount you are paid determines just how good you are at the skill you possess.

A skill can be anything from drawing, to fixing a car, to building a house or even cooking. Whatever it is, you must be good at it. And if you are really good at it, then you're good enough to teach it. Women love to learn, and if you can teach your woman something, anything of value, she will see you as a man who can produce. Remember that a woman who knows how to use tools or fix a flat tire didn't learn it on her own. More likely her father, her brother, or an ex-boyfriend taught her. A man, in other words. She will remember how to do these things for the rest of her life. So, give her a skill she can use for the rest of her life.

If she doesn't know how to fish, teach her to fish, if you know how. If you know how to fix something, make something better, know how to save money, fix a flat, hammer a nail, draw, paint, build a machine, speak another language, etc., show her and teach her how to do it. Every Seducer worthy of his salt knows a thing or two about a thing or two. And instead of filling the silence with dead air by telling her what you can do, much more can be done by showing her. You never know, the two of you could work well together and build a business as well as a relationship together. Or you can enhance the skills she already has or she could enhance yours.

The mind is designed to learn many things. It must in order to adapt and survive in any environment in which it is placed. This is the reason we have intelligence. So, do not allow your intelligence to go to waste. Use it, learn it, teach it.

***

A bag of tricks containing the above mentioned is guaranteed to make you a silver-tongued devil in no time. Women will swoon at your love songs, and they'll want you to replay them over and over again. It is a gift from nature that the fair maidens we will Seduce are moved by the words we speak. And it is also a gift from nature that man has the natural ability to use words to Seduce. If you ever wonder how it is a man below the caliber of yourself can attract and Seduce a beautiful woman, more often than not, it is because he has a way with words.

Remember, there are times when silence is best. Not every moment needs to be filled with words. You do not, under any circumstances, want to be that guy who cannot shut up. You merely want to display that you can converse, and you can converse well. Nothing is more off-putting to a woman than speaking to a man who expects her to tender herself, yet he has nothing to offer conversationally. You do not have to be the smartest, but you do have to display that you can converse like a normal human being and to be able to do this requires and shows intelligence.

When silence is golden, let it not be because you don't have anything to say. Let it come about on the way to some sort of action like holding her hand or kissing her. As stated before, sometimes the woman will employ silence to let you do your part and bridge the gap between her lips and yours. You must always be aware of such signals. They don't come because she is bored or because you have nothing to talk about. It's when she is enjoying your company. When she goes quiet and looks at your lips, and you do nothing, an opportunity may have slipped through your hands.

The ultimate goal is to make her yours. Do not feel like it is something underhanded, unethical, or secretive. It is human nature. She knows it and she expects you to know it. When you have announced your intention, dedicated your time to converse with her, and invested in who she is, she knows instinctively that you are seeking her as the reward. By conversing and not trying to bridge the gap from verbal to physical, without her ever saying that she is spoken for or not interested, would involuntarily put you in the friend zone. This is bedrock.

Technically, after meeting a woman and conversing with her, you should kiss her before you leave her. This reassures her that you are still interested in her after interacting with her. If you announce your intention, converse, but never touch her or try to kiss her and then leave her, she will be confused as to whether or not you are a fraud or if you are still into her. If she has a doubt, this allows another Seducer, who is willing to show her all the way through that he's still interested, to come in and take your girl from you. This cannot be left to chance.

It is a man's duty to go after the woman he wants. It is the responsibility of the woman to either invite your production or not. In a perfect world, it would be the other way around, where the woman announces her intention, and so forth and so on. Although this could and does happen, don't expect it because you will miss out on all the fun of laying yourself on the line for a beautiful woman. The biggest risk you can make is not taking risks especially when it comes to the opposite sex. Nothing is more fulfilling than knowing that it was your skills, knowledge and know how that has won the love of a beautiful Goddess.

INTELLIGENCE STRUCTURES INSTINCT IN A WAY TO ENSURE SUCCESS

IGNITING THE FIRE

Conversation is what defines the Seduction from its beautiful beginnings to its wonderful climax. Women love words and love to be Seduced by them. So far you have been given the tools and weapons needed to enhance not only your Seductive being, but also your Seductive success with beautiful women.

In this chapter you will be given the knowledge on how to use what you now possess in your repertoire. You will be on your way to success by <u>setting the right tone and Seductive atmosphere, having situational awareness, projecting the correct body language, fine tuning your production, protecting and providing, increasing desire and physical contact</u>.

It should be noted that instinct set in motion triggers and responses that eliminate the need for other distractions. But since we, as a human species have the rational faculty and the power of intelligence, we never rely on instinct alone, for to do so could mean immediate destruction. Therefore, we are driven by instinct, but it is our intelligence that takes this instinct, refines it, and presents it in pretty packages that women love. This is key.

Although our desire has not been misplaced, it does seem to have been looked down upon by the mass society. You shall never think women do not desire to be Seduced, loved, and/or have her inhibitions lowered. She very much does wish to fulfill her instinct to set Her Inner Sex Goddess free. She just does not want to do so for all to see, lest she be called a disrespectful name. Nor does she wish for you to put her business out there for all to see. Remember, discretion is a must, and social decorum must be respected.

It is through the artful use of words, hints, and gestures that you succeed with your lady in a social context. Then, once it is just you two alone, together you can be the animals you are by nature.

It is by creativity, intelligence, and our inherent need to know and keep secrets, that the proclivities of desirous women of the past have been kept quiet. We can speak politely of the queen who will be remembered as fair to her people for this is what was written of her. But the queen, being a very powerful and beautiful woman, still had desires as a woman. Just because she is royalty does not exclude her from having and enjoying earth-shattering orgasms. More than likely, her entire days and nights not spent in the public eye, were spent naked with suitors of her choosing. There is no need to look down on her for her pursuits of happiness for she is a woman after all, which is why this dark side rarely sees the light of day. And this is how it should be.

A woman's reputation can mean the difference between living a life she enjoys or a life filled with strife and torment. This is why it is paramount that you not

SOLOMON'S WAY III

kiss and tell. For, if you succeed with your woman, then let it be your success, not anyone else's.

Women are masters of Seduction and know how to recognize the signs of a Seduction when they come about. From the role of Seducer, it is your job to set the tone and Seductive atmosphere. You do this first by announcing your intention so the lady of your choosing is not passing you off as someone who is wasting her time. If your lady does not tell you that she is otherwise spoken for, then it is your duty to forge ahead and lay forth your production. You must set the tone by speaking to her with words to woo her, whispering to her, complimenting her, making her laugh, throwing in suggestions to what good time lies ahead and how great she will feel.

The atmosphere you create will be intoxicating to her, to say the least. This tone and atmosphere must not be broken by anything that does not ensure your Seductive success. Do not be crass, shy, belligerent, or off-kilter. Do not lose your focus.

When you are Seducing a woman, you must not take your focus from her. She should have your full attention. By making her feel special in your presence she will swoon. Do not make your production half-hearted in any way. There is no need to feel ashamed for your desires as a man. It is your birthright to Seduce and succeed with women.

There is no right or wrong time to lay siege to the woman you wish to Seduce. You decide when the time is right. You must always keep the tone Seductive by keeping the elements above present. The way you enhance the tone is by increasing your touch. At the same time while increasing your touch, you also want your woman to see the intensity in your eyes.

Women love how it feels to know that they can be taken over your shoulder at any given moment, that you could have them for lunch, that you could take them beyond limits they never imagined. This in itself is a compliment to women.

Aside from showing her your growing desire, you should also compliment her body ever so slightly in a respectful manner. The response you get will let you know how far you can go both verbally and physically.

When you touch your woman, be sure to keep it PG-13, especially in a public place. Placing your hand on her shoulders, back, knees, or arms are all appropriate for the social realm. In addition to touching your woman, you can also increase desire within her by adjusting yourself in front of her. What this means is grabbing your manhood outside of your clothes and adjusting yourself when she can see. She will believe she was the cause of such an adjustment (because of your growing desire for her) and will in turn be turned on even more. Her mind will fantasize about you and what you intend to do to her. This is always a plus.

All of these things should be sprinkled throughout your Seduction from beginning to end, starting light in the beginning and going heavy in the end. This will set and keep the Seductive tone.

* **

While the above will set and keep the Seductive tone in any situation, the Seductive Atmosphere is more about the environment in which the Seduction is to take place. Naturally, there are some atmospheres that are inherently Seductive such as weddings, private parties, pool parties, and secluded outdoor areas. Basically, any place that has romance in the air, lots of skin being shown, and/ or where it is safe and fun to get naked. Bars and places where there is dancing can also set the stage for what is to come. You should take advantage of such areas to the utmost. You can create a Seductive Atmosphere or increase one by engaging a woman's sound, smell, taste and touch. To engage a woman's sense of sight, elements of beauty should be placed around her. These things include but are not limited to flowers, work of art, bright colors, muted colors, the color red, naked women, porn and mirrors. A woman's sense of sight is far more detail-oriented than a man's. So the more effort you show, the more appreciative she will be.

To engage her sense of sound, sounds of nature, birds chirping, the ocean, the night, or music. The best music is that which speaks of love making in the songs which is what we appropriately call "love songs." A woman's imagination can be engaged easily by putting on a love song. Also, instrumental, rhythmic music, and even sounds of love making, work well for your lady.

To engage a woman's sense of smell you do not want your scent or any other to be too over-bearing, as a woman's sense of smell is extremely fine-tuned to notice even the faintest scent. Lavender is a must as women absolutely love this scent.

Other scents such as floral scents, soapy scents, woodsy scents, and even men's cologne work very well to tickle your lady's sense of smell. Be careful, though, not to put too much cologne on yourself, as it only takes a hint to do its job on the fairer sex. You also want to place scented candles around you as women love scented candles, and candles always help create a Seductive Atmosphere, as do small fires and incense.

The sense of taste has always been linked to romance from placing engagement rings in wine and food to eating whipped cream off each other's body. You should not play this down.

Women love fruit and fruit has always had an exotic/erotic appeal. So, load up on strawberries, cherries, grapes, kiwi, watermelon, and cantaloupe as well as chocolate syrup, whipped cream, honey and caramel.

It cannot be emphasized enough that the goal of your conversation and Seduction is to make your girl yours physically. This means your goal is touching her. But also, in this context, it means other things that come in contact with your girl's skin. These things should be soft to touch and inviting enough that your girl imagines being naked with this material all over her body. These things include, but are not limited to: silk, mink, cotton, soft animal fur, etc. Big soft sheets and a comforter that she could get lost in will make her love to get naked and wrapped up in them.

When all of the senses are engaged, your woman will go into sweet overload, your Seductive atmosphere having done its job in awakening Her Inner Sex Goddess.

* * *

Many men fail at the game of Seduction because they fail to take into account the current situation at hand. Being able to recognize and accurately assess situations is what is known as having situational awareness. What this means is when you spot a beautiful woman you wish to Seduce, before applying the Method you do a little analysis.

You look around her. Who is she with, if anyone? Is the person she's with a man? And if so, is the man her husband? Her boyfriend? Does she have a ring on her left ring finger? Is the man a friend, a lover, her brother, her uncle, her grandpa? Try to deduce by their interaction what the relationship is. Is she at work? Are any of her supervisors around? Any potential suitors? Are any of her girlfriends around? How do you think she is feeling? What can you deduce from her facial expressions and body language? This is where your knowledge of psychology has an important role to play. If she is with company, what is their purpose? Are they having lunch? Shopping? Hanging out, etc.? If she's by herself, what is she doing? Why might she be alone? Does she seem to be looking for company of your rank and file?

Every situation has its own list of questions you should ask yourself during analysis. Remember, you are not stalking her. You are simply taking an observational standpoint which should not take you but a few seconds. During analysis, the questions you ask yourself don't have to follow the same line of questioning as above, but they shouldn't stray too far from it. Being able to correctly assess the situation will save you great amounts of effort, where your Seduction should be effortless, and great amounts of time pursuing a Seduction that cannot be had.

Of course, analysis helps, but it should not dissuade you from Seducing the woman of your choosing. If you feel she is worth your efforts regardless of the situation or people around her, then by all means, Seduce at will. Just keep in mind that there may be more than one person you have to charm in order to Seduce your woman. This also means that there is more than her own opinion that she will consider when it comes to accepting your production. If for any reason her friends, both male and female, relatives, co-workers, etc. feel that you are bad news, they may keep her safe from you by protecting her from you both verbally and physically. This could happen for a variety of self-centered reasons. Her company may want to see her with someone else, they may judge your book by its cover and feel she is not good enough for you or you for her, they may not like the way you dress, act, talk, look, etc.

For whatever reason, it is paramount that you do your homework. Your analysis may be short. Just take in the situation, and if you see that there may be distractions, you could either wait until she is by herself or be bold and approach her. Then introduce yourself, excuse her and yourself from her company where it is just you two and announce your intention. Fortune favors the bold. And women find such boldness and confidence intoxicating.

* * *

While there are many factors to your appearance that play a part in how you come across to the fairer sex, none is more important than your body language. Projecting the correct body language is a must for the Seducer as it enhances the Seductive aura for his female companion and also makes her feel safe and cared for in his presence. Beginning with your face and head, your look should be that of relaxation and calm intensity. The reason being that women are masters of reading emotions and are also sympathetic to those emotions that she can sense. In a way, how you feel can make her feel the same way. So, if you are fearful and/or shaky in her presence, then she will feel just as uncomfortable. Your job is to come across as a strong man who can deal not only with your internal issues, but hers as well if they shall arise. She wants to know that if she becomes overwhelmed, you can calm her down and steer things in the right direction. Therefore, you shall not be shaky or shifty in her presence. Your expression should always be assured, and the effect of your expressions should always be assurance. Your head need not be tilted with your head to the sky. No one wants to look up your nose, and putting your head in this position is unnatural and awkward. You also do not want to bow your head as if in submission, because submissive is how you'll come across, and nothing could be more counter-Seductive than a submissive male. What is okay is looking down with your hands behind your back, or one on your chin or on your temple in deep contemplation. A man who can think for himself, or think in general, will always come across as Seductive to women.

Your shoulders should not be hunched up by your ears nor hunched over like a hunchback from Notre Dame. Your shoulders should be relaxed and completely unassuming. Some men's shoulders tend to lurch forward due to tight pectoral muscles. This can easily be overcome with regular stretching. A man's upper torso is his power. It is what defines him and shows dominion over all other life forms. Women understand this instinctively and love it when a man's upper torso, namely his chest, shoulders, and stomach are well defined. Though one need not go to the extreme and produce a Herculean physique, it does bode well for a Seducer to project a strong and powerful appearance.

Although it has been written in many books that one should walk completely erect with the chest stuck out and head to the sky in order to project power and confidence, such a posture is not needed, and is also unnatural, uncomfortable, and awkward and runs the risk of producing an effect that is anything other than powerful and confident. You should not be hunched over nor should you be uncomfortably erect. The midline is simply something comfortable and relaxed. Remember, you are not in a contest with your woman to show dominance and intimidation through physical size. You are simply displaying to your woman and/or women in general, that you are a man capable of fulfilling her needs, her primary biological need and her secondary general needs. Women do their part to look good for you, so you should do your part and return the favor by looking good for them. Designer clothes and having a personal sense of style will figure well into the equation, but none factors quite as well as having a nice physique woman can grab on to and fondle.

Nothing shows potential love-making skills better than a set of nice washboard abdominal muscles. Such a display shows not only that you are physically fit for the challenges life has to offer, but that you also know how to move between the sheets. Women can glance at a set of abs and easily begin to fantasize about how many orgasms you could bring her in one night. But of course, not everyone has the ability to develop visual abdominals, and although not a requirement, they do help in any sense. Women have been designed to love men, just as we love women, and so a man of any bearing can succeed. But women, especially those of high caliber and rank, want men who reflect the worth women assign to themselves. Therefore, any amount of effort is helpful in your quest. How you carry yourself and what you project goes a long way in how the female species judges you. These little things can get your foot in the door, but it is what you can produce and provide that will keep you in her bedroom.

Your gait when you walk shall always project confidence and assurance. Therefore, your stride should be smooth. Never hurried, never uncertain. The point is to provide a space where your woman can feel comfortable and carefree in your presence. In order to do this, you must maintain a sense of safety and stability for her from beginning to end. After all, you cannot expect your lady to feel comfortable and carefree around you if you cannot feel strong and confident around her.

So, relax. Show confidence, ability, assurance, and safety, and you will project the correct body language.

* * *

Outside the presence of women, you must always be working on yourself to make yourself the best that you can be. In order to have multiple successes, you must always be fine tuning your production. It is here that you take an honest look at yourself and the reactions you inspire. You shall not let your ego play a part when judging what you do rationally. A step back is all that is needed. A moment of introspection to assess clearly your behavior and the behavior you induce in the fairer sex. If you are successful, you should narrow down what you do and how you do it to key elements so you never lose sight of them or abandon them altogether. Having knowledge of what exactly you are doing in your Seductions when you are doing them is paramount as a consummate Seducer. And although you are aware of what works, this in no way means that your methods cannot be enhanced and refined to the point of perfection.

The Archer, whose skill with the bow and arrow are legendary, did not become a legend by chance or overnight. First, he had to learn the mechanics of his tools, how they moved, felt, and worked. After seeing the hows and whys, he then took his newly learned activity to still targets then those that were moving. Over time, the way his weapon was held became secondary, his focus and skill becoming primary.

He went back to hitting targets that were stationary, but this time decreasing his target area to the size of a dot. Days, months, and years were spent targeting this bull's eye until hitting it became second nature, time and experience having done their job in solidifying this skill. It is the same with the Seducer as it is with the Archer. You must take into account the tools you must work with in your field of work or profession. This would be the tools you've always possessed and/or those that were recently acquired. From there, you begin to see how each tool works and how it can enhance your performance or how you can enhance its performance.

No one starts out a Master nor does one become a Master overnight. Through trial and error does one find out what works and what doesn't. Through time and effort does one fortify his skill. Once the bull's eye has been hit many times consistently consecutively, then your form has reached Mastery. Your technique has reached Mastery. You have reached Mastery. From here every aspect should be remembered and locked into place, this posture being executed every time the arrow leaves the bow.

Training consists of acquiring a new skill and learning all about this new skill. Practice consists of mastering all that you have learned about your new skill. So, practice. Master your tools, fine tune your production, and the rewards you reap, and the skills you keep, will win the respect of all Kings and the loins of all Queens.

* * *

Some would assume that the only duty of a Seducer is to enrapture a woman's total being, to bedazzle her with your showy displays of Seduction and to finally subdue her and be rewarded with her essence for all your hard work and effort. While the above is your ultimate goal, it is not the only goal that you strive to reach. You must also give each and every Seduction, every woman whom you wish to tame, a convenient backdrop of safety that gives her the confidence and security she needs to be completely vulnerable with you. You do this by offering her a sense of protection.

Whenever a woman is in your presence and is the prize of your Seduction, she must know with every fiber of her being that she is cared for and safe from harm. The way this is done isn't through verbal displays that tell of how you would slay any three-headed dragon should they be a threat to you or your lady. You do this by showing her how confident you are in your pursuits for her charms.

Only a man who is sure of himself, and of accomplishing his goal of making a beautiful woman his, can assure her that he will provide the safety, comfort, and security that she very much needs from him. Sure, brute strength has its place, as does courage in the face of danger, but she does not need to see nor experience these things first-hand in order to know that you will protect her. Doing so too early in your courtship could have an adverse effect and could crumble completely any mountains you strived so hard to construct. Do not let your butterfly drift away over your fool heartedness.

Women have been designed to take in only a glimpse of what you have to offer visually, verbally, and physically, their minds filling the dark spaces with images from their own imagination. Women love the mysterious, and a man of mystery is sure to fill his lady's imagination with pleasurable images.

Once you have achieved your goal of projecting perfectly a perfect pose of protection, you must fulfill the other half of the equation which is providing. Providing, in the Seductive context, means providing your women with sexual pleasure in the most specific sense and providing pleasure period in the general sense.

The ultimate goal is to make her yours, but your lady will be greatly disappointed to the utmost if all your efforts culminate in a lackluster climax. As a Seducer, you must be able to provide sexual pleasure else you cannot accurately define yourself as a Seducer.

Although women are appreciative of any effort and interest on your part, it is a must that your efforts are built on a foundation of competency, skill, and know-how. A facade of a castle built from twigs and cloth

SOLOMON'S WAY III

will fly away at the slightest breeze while a castle built of stone will stand strong in even the mightiest of thunderstorms. Study the female form, her anatomy, her biology, her psychology. Refine and define your sexual technique. Etch yourself in the concrete tablet of her mind so that she will always remember you in this lifetime, and the next, as a worthy and competent lover. Make her fantasize about you, your touch, your aura when she's without you, even after days, months, centuries have long passed.

Providing pleasure in the general sense means making her feel beautiful in your presence. The great efforts you make during your Seduction must never dull and fade away in the beginning, middle, or end of your Seduction. Women never tire of hearing how beautiful they are, how smart they are, or how interesting they are. Therefore, you must never stop complimenting her on these things. Even if you know everything about your lady, you must never assume that there isn't more left to learn. Nor should you ever make her feel this way. Nothing can dim your lady's light faster than making her feel that she's no longer interesting to you. This shall never be in your Seducer's genetic make-up, even if your seduction has run its course after a long period of time. You must always provide pleasure which means providing not only what is pleasurable to the fairer sex, but also what is particularly pleasurable to your lady at hand. Always remember that a woman loves to feel understood and validated by a man. Therefore, listening and giving her feedback to let her know she has been heard and listened to is pleasurable. Sometimes it is often the simple things that get the job done that we most often forget.

CHRISTOPHER J. SOLOMON

***

Of all the tools and techniques used by the Seducer to enhance the pleasure within his female companion, none does a better job than increasing touch and physical desire.

The female of our species has been designed to be ultra-sensitive to touch. And with good reason: a woman's sense of touch is directly linked to her sex drive. Thus, a simple hand massage or foot massage or any massage in general is sure arouse sexual desire within your woman. It is for this reason women love to be pampered with spa treatments and massages. All of this acts as a natural aphrodisiac, heightening her touch receptors within her, strengthening that fierce ball of lightning inside of her brain. A woman is so linked to her sense of touch that even the slightest mention or suggestion of touch is enough to arouse desire. This is why women love romance novels, erotica, love stories, etc. They can actually place themselves as the female lead character and feel exactly what she does as if she was in the story.

These little Gems of a woman's biology shall not be overlooked. In the beginning of your Seduction, touch should be incidental, even accidental and should not be used too much as you do not want to come off as needy, desperate, or creepy. You do want to break the contact barrier early on to show that you are unafraid to be bold with her, but too much too early on can spell disaster for your Seduction before it has even begun.

After you have had the pleasure of talking with your woman, and she has given you her trust, you should increase touch smoothly without bringing too much attention to it. You do not want to seem awkward or mechanical. Therefore, you should bring up a subject that relies on physical contact, such as telling her how you found out that stress has way of showing itself in the human body by contracting a certain muscle, usually the neck, the upper back and shoulders. Demonstrate how you also learned to alleviate such stress with your hands. You can also do the same for her hands and her feet. Be forewarned! Be prepared to satisfy your woman after you give her a good rub down because she will be expecting you to tame Her Inner Sex Goddess.

Hands, feet, shoulders, upper back, and her neck are all safe zones that you can pamper in public or alone that won't seem too over-bearing, grabby or over-eager to your lady or others. Elders know what lots of physical contact will lead to, so be respectful of social decorum and know and understand what power you behold in your hands. Full body massages shall come later when the two of you are alone.

When this situation comes about, leave nothing untouched on your lady. This means from the top of her head and ears to Achilles tendon and toes and everything in between. Remember women love to be touched. It's in her biological make up. It is in our biological make up to touch. So, touch her like you mean it. It is the reason the female form with its beautiful curves are so appealing to our eyes. To make us want to pamper, adore, and arouse that Hidden Inner Sex Goddess.

SPEAK HER LANGUAGE AND SHE SHALL BE YOURS

MELTING THE SUN

The words you use have a powerful impact on the female of our species. Words should be crafted carefully when speaking to your lady or others of her kind, because women read not only the spoken words but also the facial expressions, gestures, body language and utterances that accompany them. They naturally seek congruence with what you display for them to dissect. They want to uncover not only the meaning of what you say, but also the meanings of what you didn't say and could have said.

Therefore, you must not confuse your communication with being what it is not. Your talk should make sense and you should always be aware of what you are saying to the fairer sex. Your words should always fall into certain categories: sturdy talk, flirty talk, and dirty talk. These are the categories the Seducer uses when he speaks. Nothing less, nothing more.

Sturdy talk is the talk you use when conveying solid information. It is direct, unabashed, and to the point. In the realm of Seduction, sturdy talk is used when explaining fact, giving important information, or giving direct orders. A man, let alone a Seducer, must have an extremely firm grip on sturdy talk, for it is what will silence the masses, move people, and get the job done. Saying what you mean, and meaning what you say, would be an example of sturdy talk. No man or Seducer can hope to succeed without it. Introducing yourself and announcing your intention is another fine example of sturdy talk.

Flirty talk is the talk you use while Seducing your woman. Your words are playful, imaginative, thought-provoking, and complimentary. The difference between sturdy talk and flirty talk is sturdy talk provides the framework of your Seduction while flirty talk fills the area provided. If sturdy talk provided the land, flirty talk would be the theme park that you build on this land. Nothing is taken seriously in flirty talk. It is fun and games. It is fantasy. It is enhancing the mundane. It is Seduction at its finest.

Dirty talk is what you use when you want to enhance your flirty talk to the point where you have already or are about to make love to your sweet lady. You explain to her what it is you want to do to her, how she will feel, how aroused she will be, and how beautiful her orgasms will be. Dirty talk should only be used when it is okay to do so with her. It is only meant for her to hear, not anyone else. Whispering works well when speaking dirty. Women love the fact that a man can play puppeteer with her thoughts. Doing so shows dominance which is another Seductive quality women love.

Although only three categories of talk are necessary for the Seducer, you must be completely aware of the fact that starting in one category can easily end in

SOLOMON'S WAY III

another category. And that categories can change in the blink of an eye. Sturdy can become dirty or flirty; flirty can become sturdy; dirty sturdy, etc. You must be able to flow effortlessly with the life force of the conversation. You must be able to keep a pulse on it. If you stumble or fumble for even a moment, all can be lost. Women are forgiving, but if they sense weakness or nervousness as the reason for your falter, like a beast who can smell fear, she may tear you limb from limb making your recovery impossible.

This is why you must be prepared with words that dazzle. The female of our species long to be dominated by words that come from a man's mouth. So, dominate her the way she wants to be dominated. A woman will try to throw verbal hurdles at you to see if you are quick enough to jump over them with grace. The man whose flow of conversation is undisturbed by such hurdles wins the race.

You must keep in mind that a woman's language is not logic based. It is emotion based. Therefore, the left side of the brain does not dominate; the right side does. So, when you speak to her, your words shall be those that help the right side of her brain do what it does best: think in pictures. While you speak, she is busy conjuring images in her mind. Some dirty, some weird, some completely off base from who you are, but regardless, she is still imagining. This is why you must dazzle her. Give her images to think about. While she is listening to your wonderful talk, she will be so enraptured by your spiel that she will not want to hear anything else. She will not want to go anywhere else. This is what you want of her.

Words are an aphrodisiac to our fair maidens. You can bring your lady to a raging boil and melt her resistance with your words alone. This is why you must be a master of words. You must be a master of language. You must be a master of women. Most of your talk with women will be flirty talk. It has to be, because it is the kind of talk that dominates the female psyche. Sure, questions may arise that you may have to answer in sturdy talk, but always be sure to bring it back to flirty. Else, if you keep things sturdy, then your Seduction will be inflexible and not a Seduction at all. You will drone on like a teacher teaching a boring subject. Thus, you become boring by association. Nothing can kill a Seduction faster than being boring or boring by association.

We, as men, have been gifted with the generative gene. We create, we amplify, we disturb the peace, we build castles, and swords. This is the nature that women love. So, do not stop being what you are. Some men are afraid to bring up subjects to talk about because they feel they are stupid to women, and some of these men may be right. The average topic a man wants to talk about will not be the same subject a woman will want to talk about. That is why you must keep your topics well within the realm of what is considered woman friendly as stated in the previous chapters.

Although woman friendly topics alone will aid you in your quest to Seduce, nothing helps more than speaking a woman's secret language.

Women, masters of the art of talk and communication, have evolved a sub-language that is well known to all women, but only known to the men who know how to Seduce them. This sub-language allows a woman to use ordinary words to communicate superficial ideas that the common man would pass off as banal, but at the same time she's able to speak the desire that burns within her, none being the wiser unless she's speaking to a Seducer.

The way she does this is simply by speaking to you. Women, always wanting to be chased, can only do so much before she is doing too much in the game of Seduction. This is why it is up to you to be attentive. What this means is hearing everything she is saying, the words she speaks and the words that remain unspoken. Again, women don't want to have to spell it out for you. You, being a man and having your desires for women, should understand a woman's desire to be Seduced.

She will speak her secret language through hints and suggestions, making off-hand comments or bringing up mundane topics. She will speak with gestures, generally in the direction toward you or doing things for you. She will use facial expressions, lighting up when she sees you, smiling, giving you knowing looks, letting her eyes soften when she looks at you mimicking bedroom eyes, and/or she's expressive, ultra-animated in your presence, calling attention to her eyes and her mouth. She will use body language turning toward your direction, using open arms, open legs, positioning herself closer to you or somewhere in your vicinity. She'll reveal herself to you giving you good glimpses of her naughty parts as if by accident or unintentionally. All these things should and must be picked up on if you wish to succeed with the fairer sex. This is the language she uses to show that she wants to be Seduced without being so forward. She has a whole arsenal at her disposal, but she may only use a few of the weapons to get the job done.

It is this language that most common men do not seem to understand and leaves women frustrated and complaining to their girlfriends saying, "I gave him all the signals and nothing." Women always want you to be more than you actually are. Meaning, they want you to be able to be a little psychic, a mind reader of sorts, and to be able to pull out of them what they really want to talk about. Remember, it is the Seducer's job to bring the excitement and the woman's job to be excited. You bring the fire, she will keep the heat. You bring the current, she will store the charge.

Generally, a woman does not mention a topic that she does not want to talk about. She mentions what she wants to talk about. This does not mean that the conversation must stay on this topic. It just means that this is the bait she tosses out there for you to do with it what you will. Perhaps an illustration is order.

Let's say you're talking to a beautiful lady, and you ask her, "What happened yesterday?"

And she responds with, "My car had a flat tire and I had to call my ex-boyfriend to pick me up." Now, there are plenty of conversational threads one could pull at to keep the conversation going. Any common man would keep the car as topic of conversation and thus bring about an unenterprising, boring use of words. A Seducer never leaves an opportunity like this to chance or spoils it by being boring. He first analyzes the response and recognizes that she could have responded with a simple, "I had car trouble." Instead, she gave you details when she didn't have to, and she revealed to you something else: the fact that she doesn't have a boyfriend. If she had a boyfriend, she would have called him to pick her up instead of her ex. Then, there's the fact that she even mentioned an ex-boyfriend at all. Why would she mention this to you? Because women live in the world of romance and

SOLOMON'S WAY III

relationships, and she's seeing if you're wise enough to catch on to what she's telling you.

So, being a Seducer means you immediately hone in on the fact that she has told you she is single, and you go from there. She could care less talking about her car and car trouble. You could begin by asking her how long she was with her ex, what kind of guy he was (to assess what kind of guys she goes for), how it ended, why it ended, or you could make a joke about it and elevate the conversation saying something like, "Is that why he's your ex? he couldn't show you how to change a tire, or is it because he was lame in bed?" She has given you the keys you need. All you have to do now is open some doors. It is never a bad idea to shoot straight from the hip with your questioning about her love life. Women love bashing ex-boyfriends and informing you of what kind of love she has had or is used to. She instinctively wants to know if you are going to be more of the same, or are you going to provide her with greater amounts of pleasure. These are the kinds of conversations she wants to have with you. Women love talking about relationships and all things having to do with romance. So, at some point you will have to steer the conversation in that direction if you ever expect to get anywhere. All conversations that start out with other topics should eventually lead you to her heart. This is bedrock and the goal of a Seducer's spiel.

When you have used your weapons wisely and found yourself within the realm of her heart, she will let you in and now wants to see what you can do or will do. She wants to imagine what it will be like to be with you while you explain to her what you will do to her and with her if given the chance. This is where the Seducer's energy is magnified. All that has been done and said thus far means nothing if you get to this point and falter. This is where you must sell yourself to the utmost. You must actually envision yourself taking her to heights she has never experienced before, tell her things she has never heard before, and be the man that she has longed for and fantasized about forever.

This is what separates ordinary men from Seducers. Seducers are able to pull this nature out of women effortlessly. A Seducer is able to take a response to a question, mundane topic or off-hand comment, and use it to ignite the flames of desire within women. This is what gives a silver-tongued devil his silver tongue. Once you have had plenty of success with women and you have tapped into your true beastly nature, women will be able to sense your ability just by your presence alone. It will radiate from you like an energy-field. The way you move will speak of the pleasures you have awaiting the women that you deem worthy. And this is how it should be.

It is knowing that being a nice guy and being subtle has its place when necessary, but being that fantasy figure women lust after will yield better results. There is absolutely nothing wrong with letting a woman know what you want with her. Sometimes, time does not permit the long drawn out song and dance. Therefore, you must seize the moment and capitalize. Women respect a man who can speak his intentions clearly without shame, guilt, or uneasiness. Seducers go after what they want and usually get it, because they were bold enough to go after it.

Always keep in mind the point of your conversation: For her to enjoy herself, and for you to enjoy her. You are not trying to create conflict. You are not at odds with each other. You are trying to show each other

SOLOMON'S WAY III

how well you flow in harmony with each other. She wants you to win, so win her. Let her know she can feel safe and protected with you, and you can provide the pleasure necessary to subdue her biological desire.

Goddesses are moved by words that remind them of how beautiful they are

LOVE NOTES AND LETTERS

Although the words you speak verbally have a profound impact on the fairer sex, nothing has more of an Eternal aspect than words etched into stone tablets or, in general, the written word. Women can remember words fairly well, but due to the passage of time, worldly events and experiences, those words could easily fade away. The written word, on the other hand, remains the same and has more longevity.

This is why, as a Seducer, you must utilize the power of the written word to keep your presence with her even when you are not there physically. The way you become memorable and ensure your presence is immortal is through carefully constructed love notes and letters. Love notes and love letters, or shall I say, lust notes and lust letters, are what will get your woman thinking dirty thoughts about you in and out of your presence. They are something she can read over and over again, each time bringing her to ecstasy and keeping her hot and bothered for however long she wishes.

Your notes are just short and simple reminders to your sweet lady of how beautiful she is to you, what you intend to do to her the next time you meet, how badly you desire her, how much you desire her, etc. A few choice words are all it takes to unleash Her Inner Sex Goddess. Chances to slip your woman a nice little note should never be missed. Even if you see each other all the time, you can slip your girl a note and tell her not to read it until you leave. Or you could have her read it in front of you and then tear into each other like wild beasts. It is up to you. Women love to communicate. It's what they do. And they love reading, especially the dirty stuff, so why not appease and please your woman to the utmost?

Love letters, or rightly termed lust letters, are just longer versions of love notes. These can be anywhere from one page to several pages in length. Since they are longer, you can take your time and be more descriptive in detailing full-length scenarios. Women want to get lost in your words, so give her words to get lost in. Remember, women love stories and to place themselves as the main female character. Use this to your advantage and cast her in your very own erotica novel. Let her play the distressed handmaiden and you, the valiant knight she has trysts with in the wine cellar. Or whatever you can come up with.

Do your homework. Know what your girl's fantasies are, what kind of porn she likes, what kind of erotica, etc. Women love this kind of thing. The problem is the common man is not playing with women, or their fertile minds, the way they should. This is why women resort to books and movies to get what they need.

SOLOMON'S WAY III

It should be understood that the art of note and letter writing is a lost art form. Before the days of modern technology as we know it, the only way to communicate was through letters. Women and men alike waited for what seemed an eternity to hear from their significant others. It was and still is a magical moment when one opens a letter or note. It takes the mind away from the hardships of reality for a moment. This is always a much-needed escape for anyone from the mundane. The trials and tribulations of life do not usually allow time for the mind to relax and fantasize about those things which reality does not offer. Therefore, most people find it therapuetic to find relief in books, magazines, and movies where characters get to live out lives that seem too good to be true. We live vicariously through the lives of others. But this magic can be captured and used to the utmost in the art of writing. You create the worlds you wish for you and your women.

Although the elements of fantasy and carnal bliss. should always be included in your notes and letters, these are other necessary elements that should never be omitted from your writings.

You should and must always include a sweetheart name for your beloved. It should be a name that only you have for your woman and that only you call her by. This is what will personalize your words and link you to your girl. Women may not admit it to you or anyone else, but they absolutely love it when you give them nicknames. They show possession and caring, both qualities which are narcotics to the females of our species.

You must also establish your bond as soon as possible by mentioning an event you both experienced together either recently or some time ago. Recalling a pleasurable event allows your woman to relive the experience and experience what she felt at that time over again in the present moment. This always bodes well as women love to replay events in their heads.

You must also include elements that speak uniquely to her. The things she likes to hear, the things she likes to have done to her, the things she likes to do. Just because you are not present to produce your seductive spiel does not mean that your words should not still be all about her. They very much so should still be all about her. Women want to know that you know them better than anyone else, that you are for her, and that you think the world about her. She wants to know that she very much is a part of your life as you are hers. Women long to hear how desirable she is to you and how her presence or absence makes you feel.

If you wish to make your girl smile, you should include elements that speak of the youth of your romance such as little doodles and drawings. Always include hearts and/or hearts with both of your names inside with a plus sign. Even though you two may not be in love with each other long-term-relationship wise, you do adore her, and it always bodes well to let her know this. Regardless if your dealings are lust based, you do enjoy her, and her company which has all the underpinnings of love to it. Be cautioned, though. You do not under any circumstances want to profess your undying devotion to your girl before the time is right. She will be the one who makes the call on whether you two are in love. Just because you two are matched physically does not mean you two are compatible relationship-wise. You two can just be lovers with no strings attached. Professing your heart too soon can make her run away from you. In the relationship department, men are often too eager to give women their hearts without actually assessing the parameters of their relationship. This has caused many men to leave the relationship broken-hearted. Women do want to know that you care for them and would do anything for them, but they also want you to remain strong and stoic. They do not want wimps clinging on to them like they are your only chance at love.

Women love to chase as much as they want to be chased. A woman's goal is to eventually subdue you and make you hers, but she does not want it if it is too easy. If you fulfill her sexually and you in turn become clingy, she'll abandon you as if you were a sexless male.

It is a very intricate game that men and women must play in order for both parties to leave satisfied. Your goal must be providing pleasure and protecting her. This is why you must tread lightly when putting your desires on paper. Be sure to remain cool, calm, and collected.

Digressions aside, pleasure for pleasure's sake is paramount. You can keep things fun, flirty, and sexy for as long as you wish. When she expresses the desire for more, that's when it is your decision to take things to the next level. This is how things are for the Seducer.

Other elements that can be included in your notes and letters is your scent, either your cologne that she loves to smell on you, or your natural scent. Reading a note or letter from you that sounds like you and smells like you, places you there with her. Always a plus.

Remember that your handwriting need not be fancy nor perfect, just legible. What is the point of writing something no one can read? Make your handwriting soft on her eyes so she doesn't have to struggle to read what you are saying. Sloppiness can cause confusion and ruin any kind of magical moment you were trying to create. Also, speak words she can understand. There is no need to sound high-brow and pompous. Just write well and stick to the formula, and your words shall have a lasting effect on your girl.

Cast your spell by the
light of the moon,
and your magical words will
make her swoon.

SPELL CASTING

People speak words not really knowing their power. There is a such thing as "speaking things into existence." When this happens, a spell has been cast. The realm of the Dark Arts has fascinated people from the earliest of times to present. Although people may not admit it, dealing with the Supernatural realm has always had its secret admirers. But not all spell casting comes in the form of altars, candles, potions, dragon's blood, etc. Some spell casting comes in forms most are not aware of, such as holding court.

Enrapturing women who are present, putting them in a trance with your sweet-sounding words, playing with their imagination, making them lose train of thought and track of time, can all be considered spell casting. But just because you are able to hold court does not necessarily mean you've casted a spell. What differentiates holding ordinary court and casting a spell is holding court could just be a way to pass time, cure boredom or entertain. Casting a spell involves most of the above with the added element of intent.

When you hold court with an intent, which is to make a beautiful woman yours, you are no longer just holding court. No, on the contrary, you are casting a spell to ensure that you succeed in your quest. When there is a goal in mind, you will then have a method to your madness. You will work on what needs to be worked on, have topics and subjects you will use for conversation, you will move with the flow and energy of the universe. This is what the Seducer does when he decides to court a beautiful female. He casts a spell over her, putting her in a trance, and makes her enter another realm.

This is not to say that the Seducer does not actually use the Dark Arts to actually cast spells. He most certainly does but relying on the Supernatural realm to do his bidding is not the first, nor only, method of the Seducer.

The Seducer builds his strength, first, through practice and then, from experience, he becomes a master. Only when he needs to enhance his abilities to the utmost, needs to spread his influence further than his immediate vicinity, and have the forces of nature assist him, does he call upon the Supernatural realm.

Many people just do not understand the power behind thought, direction and intent. When these things are combined and spoken into the atmosphere, those things that were spoken could actually come to pass. People are just beginning to understand man's true power and the energy he uses to affect the world around him. The society we live in these days was built and structured from the power of men's minds. They cast spells and saw them to fruition.

The power behind thought is the most important element of the three elements necessary for spell

SOLOMON'S WAY III

casting. Thought holds ideas, images, and events that when spoken into existence, or manifested in the real world, has the power to change the world and/or influence the minds of others. Thought alone has this ability.

When it comes to direction, this element is of secondary importance as it is where you will determine your energy be directed. You can never say you want something if you are not willing to exert the effort necessary for your wishes to come true. Once your thought has been seeded, direction determines what is necessary to make it grow.

Intent is the last part of the equation and completes the trinity. Once you know what your desires are, and what efforts are necessary, your intent is you actually putting everything into action to ensure success.

In your Seduction, you can have the thought of succeeding, but not have your energy directed in the right direction. You can have direction with all your effort, but not have a clear-cut idea of what you are trying to achieve. This is why it is paramount that you know what you are after.

The words you use for casting a spell either when holding court or, in the greater realm with direction, thought, and intent, can take many different forms. For the lesser realm, you can whisper your charm under your breath, you• can repeat a phrase, word, or sound. Or which is a favorite of many, you can speak a spell by rhyming two sentences. Like the Gem preceding this chapter, "Cast your spell by the light of the moon, and your magical words will make her swoon."

Rhyming words does wonders in mesmerizing the mind in general and the minds of women in particular. This is why they love poetry and songs so much. The rhyme has always had a spell-binding effect. In holding court and enrapturing your quarry, it is not necessarily needed for her to actually hear your words. Remember, words have a power all their own, and just speaking them into the atmosphere. is all that is needed to get the job done.

When casting spells away and outside the presence of your women, it might be necessary for you to fill your chosen area where you will cast a spell with reminders of your girl or woman in general: candles, her scent, her items, etc. This will help get your energy up so the words you speak enter the atmosphere more powerfully. To ensure proper release of all energy, accompanying your words with a strong orgasm would help. It is not always necessary nor feasible given your current whereabouts, but it is backup when you feel that your words are not hitting hard enough.

Ancient shamans, witch doctors, and witches of the old world, all knew too well the powerful effects of the spoken word and spell casting. People used to be cured of certain ailments, have their fortune changed and found soulmates all based on what the magicians of the past ordered. This practice still goes on today except that it is overshadowed in favor of what is cool and popular these days. It matters not, though, as some people still have the tendency to freak out over those who harness the forces of nature for their own purposes. Thus, some things are not for everyone. A Seducer does not care about the opinions of others and how they relate to him. He knows what works for him, and that is what matters most.

There will always be people in the world who are never satisfied and who believe that just because they have opinions people should listen to them. True happiness is that which makes you happy, not what makes others happy. People normally assume that many of the social gatherings we partake in on different days of the year were just there for everyone to be social. On the contrary, these great gatherings were in place so all involved could direct their energy toward a common goal. They were based on the fact of nature that energy, when directed toward a certain goal, has a greater chance of succeeding when more people participate. In those days, it was not uncommon for men and women alike to spell cast in order to find their soulmate. This is the way things were for the old world.

Always remember that just because people are quick to jump on fads and change with the times, there are those who remain unchanged. There are those people of the world who have mastered nature and themselves and have been enlightened by the wisdom of the Ancient Ones. Facts do not change no matter how much dust and cobwebs abound. Wisdom does not change. These are the things that resonate today with people as they did long ago, words that seem to have been spoken today, but were written hundreds of years ago.

Nature has locked within its structure secrets for the uninitiated, waiting for them to be unlocked and revealed. All around mortal men are keys to success, keys to their future, keys to their destiny. But man being on the incorrect path does not notice these Gems dangling before him because he knows not what to look for. That is what happens when our focus hits upon the first shiny object in our sight. We become enamored and lose sight of what is really important: enlightenment.

Once one becomes enlightened with the wisdom of the Ancients, which is knowing certain truths about nature and oneself, one not need resort to nonsense in order to succeed in Seduction or life itself. It is a natural part of our being to want to be enlightened, to be fascinated with enlightenment, and to be drawn to the flame the torch of enlightenment brings.

Man, and the elements, have always been one and the same. Man has always been one with nature. It was when he started believing that he was foreign to or outside of nature that all of his problems began. You cannot flow against something you are nor can you be something you are not.

People try to fool themselves into thinking and believing that they are what is cool and hip naturally, yet they cannot seem to understand why things never quite work out for them, why they get the short end of the stick, why things seem to go against them instead of for them. The reason is simple. You cannot force nature to conform to what you want to be. Nature can only assist you in being what you are naturally. There are no short cuts. The Ancient ones found this out centuries ago and passed this wisdom down to those who would listen. Sometimes the truth is too bland and unappealing. So, fiction becomes more attractive by comparison. Pretty soon fiction becomes mistaken for truth as any lie can become truth by repetition.

It was once thought that the Supernatural Realm with its magic, spell casting and lore were often the results of an over-active imagination until events kept happening that were beyond the scope of scientific explanation. Phenomena such as animal magnetism, thought projection, mind reading, synchronicity, premonition, etc. now all resonate as something real, yet unexplainable through tried and true methods.

SOLOMON'S WAY III

Being mindful of the fact that only so much can be explained through normal methods is being one step closer to becoming wise.

The universe works in ways not found in any book, lesson, college, university, job, or science lab. This is why we have the other side to complement our analytic, scientific mind. It is that side, which regardless of all naysayers proclaiming it does not exist, still finds its way into our hearts and minds without even trying. It is what allows us to be fearful, curious, or respectful of The Unknown. It is here that true enlightenment is found. It is here where the connection to the universe is revealed and where the Ancient Ones know they could live forever along with all the others of enlightenment.

Science and education are needed to succeed in the real world, but in order to be truly successful, the meshing of both worlds, natural and Supernatural, is needed. This meshed world provides the path on which to apply your education and science. One can know all the facts and knowledge the world has to offer, but if one does not know how, where or when to apply these facts and knowledge, then they are just useless trivia. The Universe assists nature as nature is the Universe, but on a smaller scale. Once you find your way and understand your nature to the utmost, meaning the hows and whys of your craft and knowledge, the Universe reveals to you your path on which you will succeed.

Magic and Spell Casting are how nature assists you when you are on the right path. Remember, it is human nature for a man to have desires for women. Therefore, it is natural nature assists, as it does not go against itself. Forcing the issue, whether it is your desires for a particular woman, particular riches and belongings, or a particular life, does not bode well with nature on a small scale or the universe on a large scale.

This is why the Dark Arts have been feared for so long. People have seen bad happenings involving those who practiced magic. Their bad happenings came about due to not adhering to the cardinal rule of magic: when dealing with forces of nature, you must flow in harmony with nature, never against it.

Once it was known that man had the ability to work with forces of nature for his benefit, he began to use the arts for whatever purposes he deemed worthy, whether his intent went against nature or not. This brought about the destruction of many Magicians and Sorcerers. Sorcerers, or shall I say Seducers, of the past did not all possess proper instruction nor the rules for dealing with magic. But alas, the Ancient Ones have done all the homework for you. All that is needed from you is to take heed to the instructions, warnings, and principles.

The simplified manner in which to cast a spell is to hold court with your intent to make a sweet maiden yours. Enrapture her with your presence, your words, your gestures, your appearance, your persona, etc.

If you wish to take your Spell Casting up a notch with the assistance of nature and her forces, while courting your female, you can cast a verbal spell in her presence. While you are laying out your Seductive spiel and holding court, you pause for a moment, lean in close to her and whisper in her ear, "Roses are red, green are the vines, slowly but surely I will make you mine." You should end your spell with a gesture such as kissing her on the cheek or lips, and/or handing her a rose.

If you wish to cast a spell outside of her presence, you say the same words as before while imagining her and end with an orgasm, if alone and decorum permits. Alternatively, you could end with a gesture such as writing your lady's name on a small piece of paper, kissing it and burying it in the earth. Remember, her name does not necessarily need to be on paper. It could be on a napkin, a leaf, a petal, or even written on the earth itself. So long as your intent, direction and thoughts are all aligned, you will have properly cast a spell.

The choice of words you use for each spell you cast is entirely up to you as are the different kinds of spells you choose to cast. Lastly, your lady does not need to know that you put a spell on her. Some knowledge is not for everyone. The Seducer's M.O. would be that kind of knowledge. Be wise in who you reveal your wisdom to, and your days in the land shall be everlasting.

Admiration often is not
held for the world
that everyone can see,
but for the world
that no one knows exists.

YOUR SECRET WORLD

Once you have laid siege to your woman and you have successfully seduced her, you have effectively created a world that exists primarily for you and her, your secret world.

Your secret world consists of not only all the things from the humble beginnings of your seduction, but also everything up to this point. Only the two of you are aware of what you have done to her, with her, and what she let you get away with, or have your way with. This is your secret world. The details are for you two, no one else. The reason this must be emphasized is there will be plenty of times where the focus may be elsewhere, and attention must be paid to those around you, the public.

In social settings, you must tread lightly and carefully when revealing your relations with your woman or if you should reveal them at all. This is where your secret world must be kept from everyone. Occupation-wise, such a revelation could spell disaster for her or yourself. Reputation-wise, such a revelation could have people talk in circles that influence your comfortable way of living. Socially, men and women may become disgruntled and seek to sabotage your social standing. Therefore, take heed and allow your secret world with your fair lady to exist beyond the conscious threshold of everyone else.

This is where you get to play the role of the perfect gentleman, never allowing your desires for your woman to be known to others. You speak respectfully, you entertain, you take on the role that is called of you by society and/or context. This affords you great opportunity to slip your lady notes and letters.

Your girl gets to play the role of the sweetheart, the princess, the queen, fulfilling the duties and behaviors that appease her followers. Be not discouraged if she must seem indifferent. She is fulfilling a role. Sometimes such actions are needed in order to maintain social equilibrium and status.

In the past, it was not uncommon for a woman or a man of very high social standing to carry on trysts with those of a lower social standing. The queen had her servants; the princess her instructors; the king, his handmaidens, etc. In today's world, this would be akin to the boss and one of her subordinates; the housewife and the pool boy; the actor and his maid. In every instance, the secret worlds they created existed in secrecy sometimes far beyond the grave.

You must treat your secret world with care and regard. Time and society will let you know when it is proper to reveal the existence of your relations if the existence need to be revealed at all. Until then, if there is a then, the exploits and conquests of a Seducer are not on immediate display for everyone to see.

People like to believe that if it cannot be seen, then

it must not exist. Some want to be the talk of the town, to have their whole lives on display for all to see. This way of existence is not for the Seducer. The Seducer does not rely on fortune or fame in order to live a life fulfilled. He relies on fulfilling the pleasure of women, and in this regard, she fully expects you to respect her along with your secret world together.

There is much fun to be had putting on masks and playing roles for the public to consume. You know you want her. She knows all to well that you want her. Knowing looks and glances are magnified in meaning, tender caresses are electrified. Notes and letters burn with desire enough to burst into flame.

This is the power latent in your secret world. Respect it or do not create it.

Mesmerize
HYPNOTIZE

THE HYPNOTIC EFFECT

The Hypnotic Effect is the ability to induce a trance-like state in the females that you court. This can come about in many different ways, but first let us discuss the history and background of hypnosis to give you a better understanding of what you are dealing with.

Hypnosis is the idea that a person can be put into a sleep-like state or trance, if you will and be moved to actions and behaviors through the proper use of suggestion alone. This idea has always had great appeal in the realm of human affairs as on some level or another, everyone wants to be able to control someone or someone's actions.

Most of what people can recall about Hypnosis usually entails someone holding some small shiny object, swinging it back and forth while saying the words, "You are getting sleepy, very very sleepy." Although in those times this form of Hypnosis was taken seriously and being fact, we now know today that this is known as Stage Hypnosis and is nothing more than a form of entertainment.

But it was from these humble beginnings that people began investigating the notion of putting people into trance and being able to control their behavior. And it has been found that it is possible to induce trance and hypnotize someone. While you cannot literally put someone to sleep and expect them to be fully conscious of your commands and/or presence, you can implant suggestions and verbal commands beneath the conscious threshold.

The Subconscious Mind is the part of your mind that takes in all stimuli that comes through your senses and integrates it with your thoughts, feelings, imagination, and memories. The parts that we are able to see are those that fall under the spotlight of our Conscious Mind, what we choose to focus on.

The idea is to speak to the Subconscious Mind without the Conscious Mind being aware of it, and to ultimately bring about thoughts, actions, and behaviors we want someone to have or undertake. Without the Conscious Mind being aware of what's going on the less chance of the suggestion being resisted. This idea has had both its proponents and its opponents. This is why Hypnosis falls within the realm of parapsychology and/or pseudo-psychology.

For our purposes, we will assume that the idea of Hypnosis is real, not in the order and magnitude that it has been propagated in the past, but in the sense that it is possible to induce a trance, to alter the mind in such a way that it loses its ability to focus on current surroundings and/or time and make it focus on whatever is suggested. We will be using some ideas from Hypnosis and some ideas from a more credible form of Hypnosis called NLP, or Neuro-Linguistic Programming. The latter is considered to be a waking state of Hypnosis and assumes that the thoughts, feelings and behaviors of others can be induced through the proper use of language patterns and suggestions.

In the realm of Seduction, it is paramount that you create and maintain your Secret World with your lady, and this is easy to do by using the proper words.

In order to induce the Hypnotic Effect, you must use Trance Words, Anchors, Speech Patterns, and Mirroring.

The best way to enter the mind of your woman or a woman you wish to Seduce is to use her words. These are words from her personal vocabulary that she uses to express herself. These are effectively called Trance Words. They are labeled as such because when they are used by someone else, they have the ability to induce a trance. This is rooted in the idea that everyone's favorite subject is themselves, and when she hears you speak her words, they will make her feel heard and/or that you two are just alike. Using Trance Words allows you within her mind without incurring resistance from her Conscious Mind. It is difficult to Seduce a fair maiden who is defensive to your campaigns. Therefore, this subtle technique allows you in effortlessly as she will not be resistant to something that resembles her world.

We can associate memories and pleasurable feelings to certain words and/or gestures by what is called Anchoring. Anchoring links any kind of thoughts, feelings, or memories to words and gestures.

For instance, if you can see that your girl is enjoying herself, you can link those feelings to a word of your choosing by saying something like, "This is pleasure." Later on, when you want to put her in that same state again, you just repeat the word "pleasure."

The same goes for linking these feelings to a gesture. When she is in an excited state, you can tap your temple or touch her lightly on the neck or cheek. To ensure ultimate success you can anchor her feelings to words and gestures.

Another technique that induces the Hypnotic Effect is the use of Speech patterns. By mimicking someone's rate of speech, how fast they speak the words, how often they pause, whether or not they speak on the inhale or exhale, can all be used to enter your woman's mind. Although this technique is more advanced than the rest, with practice mastery can be achieved.

Our last technique is one that uses words and body language and is effectively call Mirroring. With Mirroring, you basically make yourself a Mirror so the other person can see themselves and/or hear themselves. When your lady speaks and accompanies her words with gesture such as a head tilt, hand motion or facial expression, you paraphrase and then accompany your words with the same gesture she accompanied her words with.

Once you have used any of the Hypnotic techniques to bypass the resistance of her Conscious Mind and enter her Subconscious Mind, you can then implant your own suggestions and desires. Since you have come in under the radar using her Trance Words, Anchoring, matching her Speech Patterns or Mirroring, your subsequent words will not be met with any resistance. This enables you to use Imagery, Suggestions and Commands at will to get her to respond the way you would like.

SOLOMON'S WAY III

Whenever you suggest, you use the words could, should, perhaps, and/or maybe before you make a statement. For instance, you could say something like, "Maybe you could see us together, having dinner by candlelight and enjoying a bottle of wine in front of a nice cozy fire." This statement suggests a nice evening together while painting the picture with Imagery and the subtle command, "see us together..."

A woman expects the man to lead the Seduction from beginning to end, and that means paving the road to bliss the way you would like. A Seducer never leaves the outcome to chance nor does he ever want his woman to be confused about where things are going. She wants to know. She wants to hear those words. She wants to be led astray.

We unknowingly enter the trance state when we hear our favorite song, daydream, recall certain memories, or even while talking. We lose track of our surroundings and the passage of time as if we have been transported into the past or the future. While we muse on the possibilities, the flow of thoughts and feelings move through our minds, thus being completely unaware that it is happening. This is the power of trance.

This is the state you wish to induce in your female, where time does not exist, where the world you create and the world you share just happens as if by chance. Mesmerize, Hypnotize and your days as a Seducer shall be Immortal, Eternal, and Everlasting.

THE SECRETS ARE NOW YOURS TO KEEP

SOLOMON'S WAY III

THE TENETS OF SOLOMON

1. Strive to be the best you can be.
2. Make it a point to set yourself apart from the masses.
3. Always work hard to improve your mind, body, and spirit, your spirit being who you are, what you are, and why you are.
4. Educate yourself.
5. Educate others.
6. Teach people how to teach people.
7. Love women, for they hold the keys to eternal happiness.
8. Seek your own path. Choose your own destiny. Seal your own fate.
9. Always leave something behind for later generations to learn from.
10. Make knowledge a virtue.
11. Virtue with a little vice is key. Vice with no virtue is an appetite for destruction.
12. Be kind to those who are kind to you.
13. Making mistakes is okay. Not learning from them is not.
14. When spoken to, you shall speak. If not, you shall listen.
15. Take time to observe your surroundings. There is much to be gleaned.
16. Take for granted nothing, for tomorrow is guaranteed to no one.
17. Live life on your terms, no one else's.
18. Master your skills.

19. Master your knowledge.
20. Master yourself.
21. Be proud of your accomplishments.

ABOUT THE AUTHOR

Dr. Christopher J. Solomon is a Seducer of the highest order. He possesses a Genius IQ of 1700 agreed upon by him and the United States Federal Government, Washington, D.C. He has successfully passed every IQ test known to mankind, including those taken in foreign countries as well as those taken in the United States of America.

Dr. Solomon has been awarded numerous Honorary Doctorates from Harvard in the fields of Neurobiology, Psychology, Astrophysics, Political Science, Writing, Chemistry, and Physics.

He is Chief of the Masonic Brotherhood, a Grandmaster in the Northern Shaolin Kung Fu Bok Lum Snake System, a Shaolin Priest, and is first in line in the Royal Lineage of the Shaolin Kung Fu Empire.

He currently resides in Texas, but his home is the place where he was born, Irvine, California.

www.ingramcontent.com/pod-product-compliance
Lightning Source LLC
Chambersburg PA
CBHW021442080526
44588CB00009B/655